# From Prison

# To

# Recovering Yourself

Mary Shelden

# Dedication

I dedicate this book to God. He gave me the words to write my poems for healing.

And

Michelle McCaleb, who is an answer to my prayers and truly a great friend to me. Through her obedience to God, I feel this has literally saved my life.

## Note from the Author

Do you read the Bible? Yes, of course you do. God knew you before you were born. God has faith in you, in your journey of recovery. It's hard for anyone to heal when there is a lot of people around. Find a quiet place.

God will heal you through this book of poems and scriptures. It might hit a nerve or two. It takes three minutes to heal or to save a life. Someone, no matter what your problem is, God is your answer to your prayers.

Life has ups and downs, you have friends, do you have faith in them? Maybe? Maybe not? You have faith in God, right? God has faith in you. You took this leap of faith; you walk by faith <u>NOT</u> by sight. Your journey has potholes in it. Are you going to jump over them or walk around them? My answer to that question is, get on your knees and pray. God knows the answer, give it to God. In that pothole, fill it up with love, righteousness, peace, joy, believe, faith; God's promises to you. God will be there today, for God has everything you need. The poems I wrote will help you heal. Put God in your life. I have been where you are, let go! Let God have it!

## *Ship in a Bottle*

I'm a ship in a bottle

trapped inside and no way out.

I'm a ship in a bottle

who wants to sail the

open seas without sinking.

I'm a ship in a bottle

that sits there on a shelf.

I'm a ship in a bottle

I want the wind to carry me away.

I'm a ship in a bottle

that wants to be set free.

*Acts 27:9* (NLT)

We had lost a lot of time. The weather was becoming dangerous for sea travel because it was so late in the fall,[a] and Paul spoke to the ship's officers about it.

## *The Ship*

The ship sails across the ocean.

The ship sails through the storm.

The ships' sails sink to the

bottom of the sea.

The ship sails above all

God will see you rise again.

The ship sails to the highest.

The ship sails to God's

LOVE.

*Acts 27:28* (NLT)

They dropped a weighted line and found that the water was 120 feet deep. But a little later they measured again and found it was only 90 feet deep.[a]

## *The Storm*

The storm is the habits, the

hurts, the pain, the hang-ups.

The storm is a tornado that

will take you back to your

bad habits.

The storm is nothing to touch.

The storm is one drop of

rain that can turn into

a storm inside your heart.

The storm, you can't control it,

<u>NOT</u> without God being there

to help you.

The storm you can stop

when you ask God to help you.

The storm is in all of us.

The storm is <u>NOT</u> so big

after all, you are bigger

than the storm is.

*Psalm 50:3* (NLT)

³Our God approaches,

and he is not silent.

Fire devours everything in his way,

and a great storm rages around him.

## *The Mountain*

The mountain, we can climb so

far until we fall again.

The mountain is so tall you

can't climb it alone.

The mountain isn't as tall

or big as you think it is.

The mountain you climb

is the obstacle in the road you are on.

The mountain can be removed,

pray and it shall be moved.

Nothing can move a mountain

except for God. He is bigger

than you think he is.

*1 Corinthians 13:2* (NLT)

If I had the gift of prophecy, and if I understood all of God's secret plans and possessed all knowledge, and if I had such faith that I could move mountains, but didn't love others, I would be nothing.

## *The Sign*

The sign could be from a feather,

prayer, a picture on a wall.

The sign is from God.

The sign is from a movie you watch.

The sign is the cross that

Jesus died on for sinners

who can get a second chance.

The sign is a light so small like a speck.

The sign is a voice in your heart that speaks to you.

The sign is a leaf blowing

in the wind going around

in a whirlwind.

The sign is Jesus Christ.

He never gives up on

you or anyone.

The sign is always the cross.

The sign is **NOT** a sign unless

you look up.

Daniel 6:27 (NLT)

He rescues and saves his people;

he performs miraculous signs and wonders

in the heavens and on earth.

He has rescued Daniel

from the power of the lions."

## *The Whisper*

The whisper is so deep inside

your heart.

The whisper is so loud that

you are deaf.

The whisper is lost, you

found a way to find it.

The whisper is like the wind

blowing in the leaves.

The whisper is the sound

of rain touching the ground.

The whisper is from the dove's wing flying.

The whisper is from the

Bible.

The whisper is <u>NOT</u> silence anymore.

The whisper is in your

tears where God can hear your whisper.

*Matthew 10:27* (NLT)

What I tell you now in the darkness, shout abroad when daybreak comes. What I whisper in your ear, shout from the housetops for all to hear!

## *A Dream and a Prayer*

A dream and a prayer are no

different than night and day.

A dream and a prayer are

touching God's hands.

A dream and a prayer are like

looking in the mirror.

A dream and a prayer

are heaven above.

A dream and a prayer are giving

life a second chance.

A dream and a prayer, you get

your answer both ways from

God above.

*Acts 2:17* (NLT)

'In the last days,' God says,

'I will pour out my Spirit upon all people.

Your sons and daughters will prophesy.

Your young men will see visions,

and your old men will dream dreams.

## *Treasure*

Treasure is <u>NOT</u> gold, silver,

diamonds.

Treasure is <u>NOT</u> your house, your car.

Treasure is <u>NOT</u> your jewelry,

your belongings.

Treasure is <u>NOT</u> dreams you

have every night.

Treasure is <u>NOT</u> your bad habits

That you did hold on to.

Treasure is God, he will give

you the blessings that comes

From within YOUR HEART.

*Deuteronomy 7:6* (NLT)

For you are a holy people, who belong to the Lord your God. Of all the people on earth, the Lord your God has chosen you to be his own special treasure.

## *You Know J. C.*

You know

You know

You know J. C.

like I do.

You know J. C.

like my heart does.

You know

You know

You know J. C.

from heaven above

You know J. C.

The Savior who died for us.

You know J. C.

Who can make your tears go

away.

You know

You know

You know J. C.

Who can hold your hand and lead

you on the right path.

You know J. C.

He will always be there to answer

your prayers.

You know J. C.

Read your Bible

That J. C. is Jesus Christ

Who died on the cross for us.

*Romans 3:22* (NLT)

[22] We are made right with God by placing our faith in Jesus Christ.

And this is true for everyone who believes, no matter who we are.

# *Breakdown*

Breakdown is a part of life the

tears come down on a sad

face.

Breakdown is your heart

that is in pieces.

Breakdown is the world that

is on your shoulders

where you are carrying it alone.

Breakdown is the storm

that's within.

Breakdown is in God's LOVE.

*Psalm 34:15* (NLT)

The eyes of the Lord watch over those who do right;

his ears are open to their cries for help.

# *The Journey*

The journey is the beginning

<u>NOT</u> the end.

The journey is the road

to recovery.

The journey is meeting people

along the way.

The journey is getting half

way up a mountain and <u>NOT</u>

falling on my back.

The journey is healing one

step at a time.

*Proverbs 3:6* (NLT)

Seek his will in all you do,

and he will show you which path to take.

## *Painting*

Painting is the colors of a rainbow.

Painting is the colors of a sky.

Painting is the sunrise in the morning.

Painting is the sunset in the evening.

Painting is the clear sky at night

when the stars shine.

Painting is the painter who is

God's creation.

Painting is what you paint inside

your heart.

*Deuteronomy 33:26* (NLT)

"There is no one like the God of Israel.[a]

He rides across the heavens to help you,

across the skies in majestic splendor.

## *The Heart*

The heart can change from being

broken.

The heart can beat with time.

The heart has the love from God.

The heart can rise from evil to

good.

The heart can be hurt and also

healed.

The heart is from God.

The heart is LOVE.

The heart is fragile.

The heart can be changed.

*Ephesians 3:13* (NLT)

So please don't lose heart because of my trials here. I am suffering for you, so you should feel honored.

## *Listen*

Listen to your beating heart.

Listen to the stars that

are sparkling.

Listen to the wind blowing.

Listen to the rain hitting

the water.

Listen to the ocean waves.

Listen to the blood going through your veins.

Listen to the prayer from

a friend.

<u>JUST LISTEN</u>.

*Psalm 95:7* (NLT)

for he is our God.

We are the people he watches over,

the flock under his care.

If only you would listen to his voice today!

## *Scars*

Scars are deep inside, only

God sees them.

Scars tell a story that

only you know.

Scars, only through time,

they heal.

Scars on the outside,

your friends know.

Scars don't hurt no more.

**GOD IS A GREAT HEALER!!**

*Jeremiah 4:19* (TLB)

My heart, my heart—I writhe in pain; my heart pounds within me. I cannot be still because I have heard, O my soul, the blast of the enemies' trumpets and the enemies' battle cries.

# *Hurt*

Hurt is so deep inside

you hide it.

Hurt is a broken heart from somebody.

Hurt is the pain from a loss from

a friend.

Hurt is the anger that builds up like a volcano.

Hurt is the addiction that we did.

Hurt is obstacles that you meet on the road to recovery.

Hurt is the pain from someone.

Hurt can be forgiven.

*Acts 8:4* (TLB)

But the believers who had fled Jerusalem went everywhere preaching

the Good News about Jesus!

## *Walk the Line*

Walk the line started very thin.

Walk the line to the beginning.

Walk the line is between

heaven and hell.

Walk the line on the road

to recovery.

Walk the line from prison to

freedom.

Walk the line from night and day.

Walk the line to heaven's gate.

*Isaiah 2:3* (TLB)

"Come," everyone will say, "let us go up the mountain of the Lord, to the Temple of the God of Israel; there he will teach us his laws, and we will obey them." For in those days the world will be ruled from

Jerusalem.

# *Prisoner*

There are four walls that are

around you.

There are four walls that need

to be knocked down.

There are four walls that you

are a prisoner in.

There are four walls, one, two,

three bricks may fall.

There are four walls

DON'T BE A PRISONER in

Satan's prison.

*Galatians 3:22* (TLB)

Well then, are God's laws and God's promises against each other? Of course not! If we could be saved by his laws, then God would not have had to give us a different way to get out of the grip of sin—for the

Scriptures insist we are all its prisoners. The only way out is through faith in Jesus Christ; the way of escape is open to all who believe him.

## *3 Minutes*

It only takes 3 minutes

to change your life.

It only takes 3 minutes

to hear a prayer.

It only takes 3 minutes

from here to there.

It only takes 3 minutes

to say good-bye.

It only takes 3 minutes

to give a hug.

It only takes 3 minutes

to tell somebody about God.

It only takes 3 minutes

to say I love you.

It only takes 3 minutes.

*Deuteronomy 19:15* (TLB)

"Never convict anyone on the testimony of one witness. There must be at least two, and three is even better.

## *The Day*

The day comes when the sun rises in

the morning.

The day is a new day from the

storm.

The day is a prayer to a friend

who is listening.

The day is when the wind blows

through a bird's wing when he

is learning to fly.

The day is when you see Jesus

in heaven above.

*Isaiah 13:9* (TLB)

For see, the day of the Lord is coming, the terrible day of his wrath

and fierce anger. The land shall be destroyed and all the sinners with

it.

## *Love Never Fails*

Day has passed

night has come.

Friends will help

family will <u>NOT</u>.

The world is on your shoulders

that gets heavier and heavier.

Day comes

night goes.

The stars go

the sun comes.

It's <u>NOT</u> happy nor is it sad.

The wind blows

the wind is calm.

The wall around me caving me in

I'm broken inside

that will never heal.

The tears come

the tears go.

But never stop praying

from inside out

**LOVE NEVER FAILS.** ♥

*1 Kings 8:23* (TLB)

Then, as all the people watched, Solomon stood before the altar of the Lord with his hands spread out toward heaven and said, "O Lord God of Israel, there is no god like you in heaven or earth, for you are loving and kind and you keep your promises to your people if they do their best to do your will.

## *God's Not Done with You*

God's not done with your healing.

God's not done with your journey.

God's not done with your heart

that has broken.

God's not done opening the right

door for you.

God's not done starting your

new life with Jesus Christ

God's not done with you!!

*1 Peter 2:15* (TLB)

It is God's will that your good lives should silence those who foolishly condemn the Gospel without knowing what it can do for them, having never experienced its power.

## *Clear Sky*

The sun is bright, it's a clear

blue sky.

The baby bird learns how to

fly.

The flowers bloom with love

from above.

The water flows under a

bridge where you walk.

You're on your own journey.

The clear sky is where the

sun is shining.

The clear sky is where

heaven is at.

*Deuteronomy 33:26* (TLB)

There is none like the God of Jerusalem—

He descends from the heavens

In majestic splendor to help you.

## *Fall to My Knees*

I fall to my knees to pray

I fall to my knees to

thank you.

I fall to my knees to

find peace.

I fall to my knees

when I cry for joy.

I fall to my knees

to hear a friend's prayer.

I fall to my knees to

answer my call.

I fall to my knees

to say thank you for

all you have done for me.

I fall to my knees

*Ephesians 3:14-15* (TLB)

When I think of the wisdom and scope of his plan, I fall down on my knees and pray to the Father of all the great family of God—some of them already in heaven and some down here on earth—

## *Black and White*

Black and white are hell and

heaven.

Black and white are anger

and forgiveness.

Black and white are a black

bird and a dove.

Black and white are night

and day.

Black and white are negative

and positive.

Black is evil

white is pure.

You choose the black or white.

*Genesis 3:5* (TLB)

God knows very well that the instant you eat it you will become like him, for your eyes will be opened—you will be able to distinguish good from evil!"

## *The Man on the Cross*

The man on the cross who died

for us.

The man on the cross who was

nailed.

The man on the cross who was

pierced in his side.

The man on the cross who rose

again.

The man on the cross rose Lazarus

from the dead.

The man on the cross who healed

the blind so they could see.

The man on the cross is Jesus

Christ.

*Galatians 6:12* (TLB)

Those teachers of yours who are trying to convince you to be circumcised are doing it for just one reason: so that they can be popular and avoid the persecution they would get if they admitted that the cross of Christ alone can save.

## *I Rose*

I rose from the dirt.

I rose from a shining star.

I rose from a sunrise.

I rose from a sinner to

a great calling.

I rose from hate to love.

I rose from the darkness

to the light.

I rose to see God.

I rose to see great

things.

I rose.

John 6:39 Living Bible (TLB)

And this is the will of God, that I should not lose even one of all those he has given me, but that I should raise them to eternal life at the Last Day.

## *Life*

Life has ups and downs.

Life has obstacles you have

to climb.

Life is gloomy, you can

make it shine.

Life as you know it,

can be a storm.

Life as you know it,

God is your right hand.

Life as you know it,

prayers can be answered.

Life as you know it,

is a promise to

a friend.

Life as you know it,

Is a blessing.

*Colossians 3:4* (TLB)

And when Christ who is our real life comes back again, you will shine with him and share in all his glories.

## *A Letter*

Dear God,

You are a healer,

You have blessed me.

You have given me strength

from the heart.

You have made me from

clay.

You have given me love

that I will give to

someone else.

You have been there for

me,

and I thank you

Almighty God.

Love your child.

*2 Corinthians 3:2* (GNT)

You yourselves are the letter we have, written on our hearts for everyone to know and read.

## *Prayer from a Friend*

Prayer from a friend who is very close to you.
Prayer from a friend, their tears you hear from them.
Prayer from a friend who you didn't know.
Prayer from a friend you meet along the way from your journey.
Prayer from a friend who prayed who said it 3 times.
Prayer from a friend who became your best friend.
Prayer from a friend who they have been blessed to have you for a

friend.

*Job 42:10* (GNT)

Then, after Job had prayed for his three friends, the Lord made him prosperous again and gave him twice as much as he had had before.

## *Never Give Up*

Never give up on God.

Never give up on a prayer

from a friend.

Never give up on the love,

faith, joy.

Never give up on you.

Never give up on the blessing

from God.

Never give up on your

recovery.

Never give up on God who

will be there for you,

give you wisdom, believe.

Never give up on a friend

who needs God.

**NEVER GIVE UP.**

*Psalm 13:2* (GNT)

How long must I endure trouble?

How long will sorrow fill my heart day and night?

How long will my enemies triumph over me?

## *Hide*

Hide your feelings from God.

Hide your deep hard secrets

inside your heart.

Hide your light from God

so you won't see him.

Hide your tears from your

friends.

Hide your love from someone

dear.

Hide your addiction.

Hide your sunrise and the

sunset.

Hide yourself from everyone

around you.

**DON'T HIDE YOUR ETERNAL**

**LOVE FROM GOD.**

*Psalm 143:9* (GNT)

I go to you for protection, Lord;

rescue me from my enemies.

## *Believe*

Believe you know that Jesus heals.

Believe you know Jesus saved sinners.

Believe you know Jesus walked on the water.

Believe you know Jesus healed the blind and deaf.

Believe you know he died on the cross and rose again.

Believe you know he fed the hungry.

Just Believe.

*Proverbs 14:15* (GNT)

A fool will believe anything; smart people watch their step.

## *Step Out*

Step out of the shadows

into the light.

Step out of the evil inside

your heart.

Step out of the shadows into

heaven's gate.

Step out of the prison walls.

Step out of the darkness where Satan has you

by the arm.

Step out of the shadows

God will be there

with that light.

*Psalm 37:23* (GNT)

The Lord guides us in the way we should go

and protects those who please him.

# *Empty*

Empty is like a page with

no words.

Empty is like <u>NO</u> love in

your heart.

Empty is like <u>NO</u> water in

a well.

Empty is like <u>NO</u> friends

in your life.

Empty is like <u>NO</u> stars

in the night sky.

Empty is like loneliness

that surrounds you.

DON'T BE EMPTY

FILL IT WITH

GOD'S LOVE.

*Deuteronomy 32:47* (GNT)

These teachings are not empty words; they are your very life. Obey them and you will live long in that land across the Jordan that you are about to occupy."

## *Take My Mask Off"

Take my mask off so

you can see my tears.

Take my mask off for

you, God.

Take my mask off of

the deep pain

deep inside.

Take my mask off so

I can take the chains

that hold me down.

Take my mask off so

I can shine.

Take my mask off so

my friends see me.

Take my mask off so

they can see the

change in me.

*Matthew 10:26* (GNT)

Whom to Fear

"So do not be afraid of people. Whatever is now covered up will be uncovered, and every secret will be made known.

## *Beauty*

Beauty is a flower blooming

within us.

Beauty is a friend praying

for you.

Beauty is the sunrise

for a new day.

Beauty is the stars

sparkling.

Beauty is the sunset.

Beauty is the love

you give us.

Beauty is the song in

our hearts.

Beauty is that Jesus

rose again.

*1 Peter 1:24* (GNT)

As the scripture says,

"All human beings are like grass,

and all their glory is like wild flowers.

The grass withers, and the flowers fall,

## *Footsteps*

Footsteps are steps that

you walk on the path

of your journey.

Footsteps are in the sand

where God is walking

with you.

Footsteps are your grace

from God

Footsteps are the friends

that walk with you

when you need them.

Footsteps are going to

heaven.

*Luke 4:11* (GNT)

It also says, 'They will hold you up with their hands so that not even your feet will be hurt on the stones.'"

# *Beginning*

Beginning is the day he

created the heaven and

earth.

Beginning is the journey

you are taking.

Beginning is the start

of a new life.

Beginning is never ending.

Beginning starts with

God.

Beginning of time that

never stands still.

*Romans 16:25* (GNT)

Concluding Prayer of Praise

Let us give glory to God! He is able to make you stand firm in your faith, according to the Good News I preach about Jesus Christ and according to the revelation of the secret truth which was hidden for long ages in the past.

## *You Say*

You say I'm strong

but I'm weak.

You say I'm loved

I can't feel a thing.

You say I have friends

I'm alone.

You say there is a God

I believe.

You say a prayer

I get an answer.

You say I have faith

I can heal.

You say don't be afraid

I say I'm <u>NOT</u>.

*1 Corinthians 2:13* (GNT)

So then, we do not speak in words taught by human wisdom, but in words taught by the Spirit, as we explain spiritual truths to those who have the Spirit.[a]

## *My Thoughts*

My thoughts are wondering

around in circles.

My thoughts are just going

many different ways that

I can't think of what I need

to do for myself.

My thoughts no one writes me.

My thoughts Satan has got he

will <u>NEVER</u> have.

My thoughts when I sleep

are dreams.

My thoughts are my own.

My thoughts are of God.

*Isaiah 55:8* (GNT)

"My thoughts," says the Lord, "are not like yours,

and my ways are different from yours.

## *I Am Broken*

I am broken can be fixed

by God's love.

I am broken empty inside.

I am broken lost but

found.

I am broken starving for

God's word.

I am broken and happy

that I shine.

I am broken silence God's

voice inside my heart.

I am broken <u>NEVER</u>

again will I be.

*Proverbs 15:13* (NIV)

A happy heart makes the face cheerful,

but heartache crushes the spirit.

## *My Tears*

My tears hurt with pain.

My tears are from having

someone tell me lies.

My tears have fallen.

My tears never go away.

My tears are nothing.

My tears are caught by

angel's wings.

My tears are carried to Jesus'

hands.

My tears are answered prayers.

My tears are my own tears

**And NO ONE ELSE'S PAIN!!!!**

*Revelation 7:17* (GNT)

because the Lamb, who is in the center of the throne, will be their shepherd, and he will guide them to springs of life-giving water. And God will wipe away every tear from their eyes."

## *Anchor*

Anchor is God's hand.

Anchor is the rope you

hang on to.

Anchor is the chains that break you.

Anchor is the rainbow

that God promised.

Anchor is the soul of

hope.

Anchor is to believe

in God.

Anchor is the mistakes

you have made.

Anchor is the second

chance.

Anchor is the love

that God gave you.

Anchor is to forgive

someone.

Anchor is the hugs

you give a friend.

Anchor is you

letting GO!!

*Hebrews 6:19* (GNT)

We have this hope as an anchor for our lives. It is safe and sure, and goes through the curtain of the heavenly temple into the inner sanctuary.

## *Candlelight*

Candlelight flickers in the window

it will guide you home.

Candlelight flickers on your right

path.

Candlelight flickers in my heart

from the love of God.

Candlelight flickers is the

Holy Spirit.

Candlelight flickers in the

storm.

Candlelight flickers from a

lighthouse that brings

you out of the storm.

*Matthew 12:20* (GNT)

He will not break off a bent reed,

nor put out a flickering lamp.

He will persist until he causes justice to triumph,

## *Silence*

Silence is words with

no sound.

Silence is love with

no feelings.

Silence is rain with

no storm.

Silence is sun with

no shine.

Silence is stars with

no sparkle.

Silence is a heart

with no beat.

Silence is your journey

with no addiction.

*Psalm 39:2* (GNT)

I kept quiet, not saying a word,

not even about anything good!

But my suffering only grew worse,

## *Circle of Life*

Circle of life takes me

to the beginning and

ending.

Circle of life takes me

to the beginning of

my journey.

Circle of life is you

are born and you die.

Circle of life is walking

around in circles.

Circle of life is a healing

preparation.

Circle of life starts with

your heart ends in

heaven.

*Matthew 10:39* (GNT)

Those who try to gain their own life will lose it; but those who lose their life for my sake will gain it.

## *The Empty Chair*

The empty chair where my

mom used to sit.

The empty chair where my

memories are.

The empty chair where she

used to rock me to

sleep.

The empty chair where

her spirit is still there.

The empty chair is

now gone.

The empty chair is now

in my memories.

The empty chair is

now where Jesus sits.

*1 Peter 1:18* (GNT)

For you know what was paid to set you free from the worthless manner of life handed down by your ancestors. It was not something that can be destroyed, such as silver or gold;

## *My Mom*

My mom was my rock.

My mom was always

there for me.

My mom and I laughed

until we cried.

My mom is alright in

heaven.

My mom will always

be there by my side.

My mom is an angel

that got her wings.

My mom is in my

memories and my heart.

*John 19:27* (GNT)

Then he said to the disciple, "She is your mother." From that time

the disciple took her to live in his home.

## *Time*

Time is the hands on a clock.

Time is a grain of

sand.

Time is a sunrise to

sunset.

Time is never enough

hours, minutes, in a

day.

Time is a drop of rain.

Time is a heart beating.

Time is the journey you

are going on.

Time is how many days are in a year.

Time is spending it

with God.

Time is when Jesus died.

Time has no ending.

*2 Corinthians 6:2* (GNT)

Hear what God says:

"When the time came for me to show you favor,

I heard you;

when the day arrived for me to save you,

I helped you."

Listen! This is the hour to receive God's favor; today is the day to be saved!

## *Mirror*

Mirror is not my face

that I see.

Mirror is not of anyone

I know.

Mirror is just a reflection

of a child.

Mirror is just another

world of Satan's prison.

Mirror is looking inside

yourself.

Mirror is God's reflection

of who he wants you

to be.

Mirror is heaven's place.

Mirror is an escape.

Mirror is hanging

on the wall.

*James 1:23* (GNT)

If you listen to the word, but do not put it into practice you are like people who look in a mirror and see themselves as they are.

# *My Own World*

My own world with stars shinning in a midnight sky.

My own world is my own memories.

My own world is a clear blue sky.

My own world is sailing the blue sea.

My own world is letting me be free.

My own world is not gloomy always sunny.

My own world is with God.

My own world where

the water flows.

My own world is flowers

blooming.

*Colossians 1:16* (GNT)

For through him God created everything in heaven and on earth, the seen and the unseen things, including spiritual powers, lords, rulers, and authorities. God created the whole universe through him and for him.

# *Satan*

Satan is a liar.

Satan can hurt you

and tell you everyone

is ok.

Satan will be the world

on your shoulders.

Satan will grab you

by the throat and

never let go.

Satan knows that Jesus

does miracles.

Satan don't like the

blood of Jesus.

*Matthew 16:23* (GNT)

Jesus turned around and said to Peter, "Get away from me, Satan! You are an obstacle in my way, because these thoughts of yours don't come from God, but from human nature."

## *Poems*

Poems are feelings written

on paper.

Poems are written in

the Holy Bible.

Poems are written in

many different ways.

Poems are sad, happy

about relationships.

Poems are deep within.

Poems are from God's

special place from

the heart.

*Psalm 149:1* (GNT)

Praise the Lord!

Sing a new song to the Lord;

praise him in the assembly of his faithful people!

## *The House that is Built on Love*

The house that is built on love

from formation to heaven.

The house that is built on

God's holy land.

The house that is built on

memories.

The house that is built with

stones that friends

have thrown at you.

The house that is built with

a floor you kneel on to

pray for God.

The house that is built by

God's love.

*Matthew 7:24* (GNT)

"So then, anyone who hears these words of mine and obeys them is like a wise man who built his house on rock.

# *Luggage*

The luggage we carry is

pain.

The luggage we carry is

the world on our shoulders.

The luggage is Satan's

lies.

The luggage is the storm

that is built inside.

The luggage is the mistakes.

The luggage is the

patient love.

The luggage is truth

belief of God.

The luggage you

Don't have to carry <u>no</u> more.

*Psalm 38:4* (GNT)

I am drowning in the flood of my sins;

they are a burden too heavy to bear.

## *Song in Your Heart*

Song in your heart is from God.

Song in your heart is the love,

hope, faith.

Song in your heart is from

Psalms.

Song in your heart is a poem.

Song in your heart is from

prison to recovering yourself.

Song in your heart is the

prayer.

Song in your heart is from

laughing, hugs, beauty.

Song in your heart is from

your story that's deep

inside.

*Isaiah 49:13* (GNT)

Sing, heavens! Shout for joy, earth!

Let the mountains burst into song!

The Lord will comfort his people;

he will have pity on his suffering people.

## *What I Used to Be*

What I used to be without God.

What I used to be without friends.

What I used to be a prisoner in Satan's prison.

What I used to be nothing.

What I used to be a seed.

What I used to be a nonbeliever.

What I used to be unsaved.

What I used to be homeless.

What I used to be was a drug dealer.

Now I am somebody.

Amen.

*2 Timothy 3:16* (GNT)

All Scripture is inspired by God and is useful[a] for teaching the truth, rebuking error, correcting faults, and giving instruction for right living,

## *Burn the Bridge*

Burn the bridge of your hurting

heart.

Burn the bridge you walked

across on your journey.

Burn the bridge that the enemy

built.

Burn the bridge of your addiction

that you don't need.

Burn the bridge of the hurt

of someone who is now your friend.

Burn the bridge of your mistakes

and your compulsive behavior.

Burn the bridge of your past,

give it to God

Cause there is <u>NO</u> yesterday.

*Isaiah 30:27* (ERV)

Look! The Lord is coming from far away. His anger is like a fire with thick clouds of smoke. His mouth is filled with anger, and his tongue is like a burning fire.

## *Different*

I may be different on the outside. So, I look in the mirror. God made me that way, it don't bother me. Maybe I am different on my journey that is just for me. God made my heart beautiful to bloom in God's eyes.

*2 Chronicles 15:4* (ERV)

But when the Israelites had trouble, they turned again to the Lord, the God of Israel. They looked for him and found him.

# *Healing Will it be Enough*

Healing will it be enough

from God above?

Healing will it be enough

from an answer from a

Prayer?

Healing will it be enough to

shine like a star?

Healing will it be enough from

a rainbow that was a promise

from God?

Healing will it be enough from

choices?

Healing will it be enough to be

beautiful inside?

Healing will it be enough from

loving someone?

Healing will it be enough to have second chances in your life?

Healing will it be enough?

*Exodus 15:26* (ERV)

He said to him, "I am the Lord your God. If you listen to me and do what I say is right, and if you obey all my commands and laws, then I will not give you any of the sicknesses that I gave the Egyptians. I am the Lord who heals you."

## *I'll Be Okay"

I'll be okay my friends thought.

I'll be okay <u>NOT</u> on the inside

where they can't see the tears.

I'll be okay God knew there

was hurt, and pain.

I'll be okay with a fake

smile on my face.

I'll be okay as long as

God is there with me.

I'll be okay when my journey

ends at heaven's gate.

*Revelation 4:11* (ERV)

"Our Lord and God!

You are worthy to receive glory and honor and power.

You made all things.

Everything existed and was made because you wanted it."

## *Someone Hurts*

Someone hurts you breaks

your heart that tears you

alive inside.

Someone hurts you the love

in their hearts is <u>NOT</u> filled.

Someone hurts let it go give

it to God.

Someone hurts your best

friend knows you are hurt

from someone that hurt you.

*Acts 8:4* (ERV)

⁴They were scattered everywhere, and in every place they went, they

told people the Good News.

## *The Door*

The door God is knocking at in

your heart.

The door you open up your

feelings are out.

The door to salvation, wisdom

and truth.

The door to the righteousness

is from God.

The door to the truth, the way

and the life.

*Matthew 7:7* (ERV)

Ask God for What You Need

"Continue to ask, and God will give to you. Continue to search, and

you will find. Continue to knock, and the door will open for you.

## *Break the Bondage*

Break the bondage of our
chains that Satan put on us.
Break the bondage of our
addiction.
Break the bondage of the
prison walls.
Break the bondage of your
Heart that's in hurt,
and in pain.
Break the bondage from the
enemy who stuck you in
chains.
You broke the bondage
of the enemy.
*Hebrews 13:3* (ERV)

Don't forget those who are in prison. Remember them as though you were in prison with them. And don't forget those who are suffering. Remember them as though you were suffering with them.

## *Stone*

Stone is what the commandments

were written on.

Stone is to build your house

from the foundation.

Stone is <u>NOT</u> the addiction

we were on.

Stone is <u>NOT</u> to be thrown

at it won't break my

bones God is my protection

for me.

Stone is to make a bridge

and burn it after you cross it.

*Matthew 24:2* (ERV)

He asked them, "Are you looking at these buildings? The fact is, they will be destroyed. Every stone will be thrown down to the ground. Not one stone will be left on another."

## *Haven't Seen You Yet*

Haven't seen you yet? When you were born.

Haven't seen you yet? When you preached.

Haven't seen you yet? When you got saved.

Haven't seen you yet? When you feed the hungry.

Haven't seen you yet? When you died on the cross.

Haven't seen you yet? When you rose.

Haven't seen you yet? Jesus Christ.

*1 Corinthians 13:12* (ERV)

It is the same with us. Now we see God as if we are looking at a reflection in a mirror. But then, in the future, we will see him right before our eyes. Now I know only a part, but at that time I will know fully, as God has known me.

## *Almost Home*

Almost home these miles are

too long to travel.

Almost home too many obstacles

are in the road.

Almost home to heaven's gate.

Almost home to God's arms.

Almost home to the man on

the cross.

Almost home to the man that

healed us.

Almost home to a new place.

Almost home it's time to go.

*Hebrews 13:14* (ERV)

Here on earth we don't have a city that lasts forever. But we are waiting for the city that we will have in the future.

## *The Emotions*

The emotions are feelings that are

up and down.

The emotions are being happy

who make you laugh.

The emotions are God's love.

The emotions are the colors in

the sky.

The motions are when Jesus

died on the cross.

The emotions are going out your

front door praise God for

another day.

The emotions are the song of

Psalms.

The emotions are the full moon

at night.

The emotions are getting a

new life.

The emotions are tears in

your friend's eyes.

*Romans 12:21* (ERV)

Don't let evil defeat you, but defeat evil by doing good.

## *Dust to Dawn*

Dust to dawn I had to fall

God lifted me up.

Dust to dawn from nothing to

love.

Dust to dawn you live inside

of me.

Dust to dawn from Satan to

God's hands.

Dust to dawn from darkness

into the light.

Dust to dawn from sunrise

to sunset.

Dust to dawn beginning to end.

Dust to dawn it's just the

beginning of a brand new day.

*Matthew 10:14* (ERV)

And if the people in a home or a town refuse to welcome you or listen to you, then leave that place and shake the dust off your feet.[a]

## *Nobody's Lives Are the Same*

Nobody's lives are the same we

are different on the outside.

Nobody's lives are the same we

are different the way

we walk, talk.

Nobody's lives are the same we

are different like the sunrise

and sunset.

Nobody's lives are the same we

are different like shining stars

in the midnight skies.

Nobody's lives are the same our

paths are different and at the

end we all will be at the

heaven's gate one day.

*1 Thessalonians 4:12* (ERV)

If you do these things, then those who are not believers will respect the way you live. And you will not have to depend on others for what you need.

## *Everyone Comes Alive*

Everything comes alive God

took your heart and lifted

you up from nothing to a

shimmering star.

Everything comes alive only

through faith, believe, trust

in God.

Everything comes alive through

the Holy Spirit.

Everything comes alive when

God forgives you from your

sins.

Everything comes alive when

you let go from the past.

*Psalm 41:2* (ERV)

The Lord will protect them and save their lives.

He will bless them in this land.

He will not let their enemies harm them.

## *Cry Out*

Cry out to God for forgiveness.

Cry out for help from your tears

from a broken heart.

Cry out to God for a friend he

needs to protect in this

time of need.

Cry out for help when you

have been bullied or

scared having no friends

to talk to.

Cry out for help for an answer

to a prayer.

Cry out to the Lord, for I am

Not worthy of you.

*Psalm 5:2* (NLT)

Listen to my cry for help, my King and my God,

for I pray to no one but you.

## *God's Got Me*

God's got me by the hand to take this hard journey he will <u>never</u> let go of your heart.
God's got me from my head to my toes. God protects me by my ears, eyes and my heart.
God's got me wherever I go I never had a place of my own.
God's got me from when I was born to the day I see Him. God has my hand, heart.
If I break God can fix me.
If I cry God has a shoulder.

I can cry on. God gives

second chances.

*Micah 6:8* (ERV)

Human, the Lord has told you what goodness is.

This is what he wants from you:

Be fair to other people.

Love kindness and loyalty,

and humbly obey your God.

## *Symphony*

Symphony is songs from

voices that sing from

the heart that echoes to

God's ears.

Symphony is words written

in a song from the soul.

Symphony is a new day that

begins with a sunrise gracefully,

joyfully, a day that God has

symphony in his church.

*Acts 16:25* (ERV)

About midnight Paul and Silas were praying and singing songs to God. The other prisoners were listening to them.

## *What's Missing in your Life*

What's missing in your life?

God's eternal love, his promises at the end of a rainbow.

What's missing in your life?

The light on my path that

will show me the way, the

Truth, and the life.

What's missing in your life? Joy,

peace, love, believe, in God.

What's missing in your life?

Believing in yourself. God does.

What's missing in your life? A

friend that cares, who stands

beside you when you need

them the most.

What's missing in your life?

The love that you missed from

someone who cares and is <u>NOT</u>

here anymore.

What's missing in your life?

The strength from Christ.

What's missing in your life?

The calling of God who

whispers in your ear.

*Psalm 23:6* (NLT)

Surely your goodness and unfailing love will pursue me

all the days of my life,

and I will live in the house of the Lord

forever.

## *Arms Wide Open with Love*

Arms wide open with love

Jesus died on the cross.

Arms wide open with love

Jesus who was born in

Bethlehem under a shining

star.

Arms wide open with love

Jesus preached to his people,

made water into wine, fed

the hungry and they weren't

thirsty no more.

Arms wide open with love

Jesus nailed to the cross.

Arms wide open, he gave us

a hug and died.

*Isaiah 65:2* (TPT)

Day after day I have *graciously* outstretched my hands

to a people who turned their backs to me,

whose way of life is corrupt,

who insist on going their own way.

## *Yesterday, Today, and Tomorrow*

Yesterday is gone, we will

never get it back.

Today you are living in the

moment <u>not</u> the next.

Tomorrow isn't here yet when

God will let you know that it

will be blessed, so don't

worry about this day, it will

come soon enough.

Yesterday, today, tomorrow,

these times, <u>not</u> tomorrow

it isn't here yet. It could

Be worse or good things.

*Hebrews 13:8* (TPT)

Jesus, the Anointed One, is always the same—yesterday, today, and

forever.

## *No One Knows Me*

No one knows me except for

God above.

No one knows me except my

friends.

No one knows me **NOT** the

people in my past.

No one knows me they really

don't know me.

No one knows me take the

mask off and they will

know you like God does.

*Joshua 24:14* (ERV)

Then Joshua said to the people, "Now you have heard the Lord's words. So you must respect the Lord and sincerely serve him. Throw away the false gods that your ancestors worshiped. That was something that happened a long time ago on the other side of the Euphrates River and in Egypt. Now you must serve only the Lord.

## *Holy Spirit*

Holy Spirit is the person
Who lives inside your heart.
Holy Spirit is like a light rain.
Holy Spirit is like a star falling
and catching it.
Holy Spirit is like a candlelight
in the window.
Holy Spirit is a poem
somewhere within.
Holy Spirit is a song
someone wrote.
Holy Spirit is a time that
Has <u>NO</u> ending.
Holy Spirit was with Jesus
Who died on the cross.
Holy Spirit is there when
you get baptized.
Holy Spirit is there at the 3 crosses
that you see.

Ephesians 1:13-14 (NLV)

The truth is the Good News. When you heard the truth, you put your trust in Christ. Then God marked you by giving you His Holy Spirit as a promise. The Holy Spirit was given to us as a promise that we will receive everything God has for us. God's Spirit will be with us until God finishes His work of making us complete. God does this to show His shining-greatness.

## *Amen*

Amen is at the end of

a prayer.

Amen is having the Holy

Spirit.

Amen is having friends.

Amen is having the

faith.

Amen is having God.

Amen is the time.

Amen is Jesus Christ

Who died for us.

Amen is going to

Heaven.

Amen is recovering.

Amen is the journey.

Amen is building the

House of God.

## AMEN

Galatians 1:3-5 (TLB)

³May peace and blessing be yours from God the Father and from the Lord Jesus Christ. ⁴He died for our sins just as God our Father planned, and rescued us from this evil world in which we live. ⁵All glory to God through all the ages of eternity. Amen.

## About the Author

God gave me a gift of healing. I started writing poems when I was in jail. I wrote about how I felt beyond four walls. Nothing could tear them down except for me. I prayed every night, crying my eyes out, until I fell asleep. God listened to my heart of pain. One day these two church ladies came and visited the girls in jail and had a Bible study.

I was blessed to meet one of the church ladies, her name is Michelle McCaleb. I told her I was homeless and when I got out of jail, I had no place to go. Michelle prayed to God three times, "Don't let Mary Shelden be homeless. Don't let Mary Shelden be homeless. Don't let Mary Shelden be homeless." On January 5, 2020 I got out of jail early that morning, around 12:30 a.m. I went to find my car. When I got my car back, I didn't know where to go, but I ended up at Michelle's church.

I heard God telling me in a whisper inside my heart to go find Michelle. I don't know how I got to church that morning. I tried to sleep in my car, but I couldn't. I found Michelle. It took three minutes to find her. She found me instead. Michelle's prayer was answered. I went into a women's hope center where I started to write more poems. God's gift to me is a blessing.

From Prison to Recovering Yourself

ISBN: 9798601976985

www.galahbookstore.com

Thank you, Laura Patterson for allowing us to use your painting for the cover. You may reach Laura Patterson through the email

galahbookstore@gmail.com

New Living Translation (NLT)

*Holy Bible*, New Living Translation, copyright © 1996, 2004, 2015 by Tyndale House Foundation. Used by permission of Tyndale House Publishers, Inc., Carol Stream, Illinois 60188. All rights reserved.

Living Bible (TLB)

The Living Bible copyright © 1971 by Tyndale House Foundation. Used by permission of Tyndale House Publishers Inc., Carol Stream, Illinois 60188. All rights reserved.

Easy-to-Read Version (ERV)

Copyright © 2006 by Bible League International

The Passion Translation (TPT)

The Passion Translation®. Copyright © 2017 by BroadStreet Publishing® Group, LLC.
Used by permission. All rights reserved. thePassionTranslation.com

New Life Version (NLV)
Copyright © 1969, 2003 by Barbour Publishing, Inc.

## Coming Soon...

*Let It Go, Hang It Up, & Let It Dry*

Made in the USA
Columbia, SC
02 June 2021